# IF FOUND, PLEASE RETURN TO:

NAME _____

EMAIL _____

**"Without counsel plans fail, but with many advisers they succeed."**

— Proverbs 15:22

# COLLEGE

*Highlight*

A Journal for College Planning

DARRIEN RICE

# A special shoutout to those who helped me along the way!

BRENDA RICE

VIRGINIA "GIGI" GRAHAM

AMANDA DEPALMA

BRIANNA PENNEY

RUFFINO VALENCIA

SHANNON CHRISTOPHER

LENNON PROTHRO-JONES

FAITH-FUELED-FITNESS

FREEPIK.COM

UNSPLASH PHOTOS BY:

KARI SHEA

ADI GOLDSTEIN

KIMBERLY FARMER

MATT RAYLAND

ASMI PAI

AMAN UPADHYAY

JOHNSON WANG

ALLIE SMITH

JESSICA LEWIS

JON TYSON

PRATEEK KATYAL

SEAN KOWAL

BRIANNA SANTELLAN

# Welcome

Choosing a college can be intimidating. **College Highlight** will guide the preparation/organization necessary for you to make a good decision about college.

**College Highlight** is an all-encompassing tool to assist in answering common questions, providing organized key information, and reducing the need to spend hours on the internet. This self-guided journal, with easy-to-understand wording, will be your college planning companion and help you smoothly transition into college. It's your resource for reliable, up-to-date information on anything from terminology to how to choose a college that will be a good fit for you.

I

can

do

this

all

day ...."

— CAPTAIN AMERIC

# TABLE OF CONTENTS

# About the Author

# DARRIEN RICE-

a graduate of UC Berkeley's College Admissions and Career Planning Certificate Program 2018 cohort—is passionate about college advising. His B.S. in Human Resource Development *(Oakland University, 2003)* and subsequent M.A. in Training and Development *(Oakland University, 2008 cum laude graduate)* led to his impact on students at private and public universities across the country.

Rice's versatile work includes large-scale staff trainings and individualized student academic advising. Rice, a first-generation student, has an exceptional ability to connect with students thanks to his involvement in pop culture and fifteen years of direct educational work.

# Terms to Know

**ACT** *aka American College Test*
Similar to the SAT, this is a four-part test that colleges look at. English, math, reading, and science are tested with this one. The ACT has an essay section that is optional.

**APRIL 1ST NOTIFICATION DATE**
On this day, most universities mail out college decisions to applicants.

**AP** *aka Advanced Placement*
These are subject tests that are taken in May by students who are enrolled in Advanced Placement (AP) courses. They are scored on a scale of 1-5. If a student passes with a 3, 4, or 5, these tests often help students place out of general education and freshman-year classes, which can save up to a few thousand dollars! These scores can be considered during application reviews.

**ARTICULATION AGREEMENT**
An understanding between a two-year and a four-year college to transfer credits from one to the other. It outlines what classes can apply toward a bachelor's degree.

**ASSOCIATE'S DEGREE** *aka Associate of Arts or Associate of Science*
Two-year degree that is offered at the community college level. An Associate of Arts or Associate of Science will suffice for the technical/professional fields. Will include most, if not all, general education/basic-level courses when transferring to a four-year university.

**BACHELOR'S DEGREE** *aka Bachelor of Arts (B.A.) or Bachelor of Science (B.S.)*
This degree can be completed within four to five years. Bachelor of Arts is the mixology of roughly 33 percent Liberal Arts/General Education classes, 33 percent within the major, and 33 percent electives. Bachelor of Science mostly consists of upwards of 50 percent related classes within the major and less courses out.

**CLASS RANK**
This number is a way to compare your academic achievements with your classmates. The number often comes from a weighted/unweighted GPA.

## COALITION APPLICATION
This is a general application that is accepted at 140+ colleges and universities that are in the Coalition for Access, Affordability, and Success.

## COLLEGE APPLICATION ESSAY
Part of the college application that includes an essay you (and no one else) wrote. Prompts can be specific or vague, and they ask you to talk about yourself in the essay. This is also called a "personal statement."

## COMMON APPLICATION
This is a general application that is accepted at almost 700 colleges and universities that are a part of the Common Application Association. You only need to fill it out once!

## COST OF ATTENDANCE
How much school will cost. This price includes tuition, housing, food, and other expenses like books, transportation, a personal computer, etc.

## CSS PROFILE
Form private colleges sometimes want that asks for financial information.

## DATA COMMON SET
This is a collection of accurate, updated data for students to learn about rankings and popular publications. This comes from the Common Data Set Initiative.

## DEFERRED ADMISSION
When a college or university agrees to let you in later than the original start date (usually up to one year later).

## DEMONSTRATED FINANCIAL NEED
The remaining cost a student needs for college. Cost of Attendance (COA) – Expected Family Contribution (EFC) = Demonstrated Financial Need.

## DUAL DEGREE
Admission to dual-degree programs, in which students ultimately receive a bachelor's degree and an advanced degree. A dual degree differs from a dual or double major, in which students receive one degree in two different concentrations. At the end of this route, you get a bachelor's degree and one other more advanced degree, such as a master's degree or a Ph.D. This is different from double majoring, which means a student gets one bachelor's degree in two subjects.

## EARLY ACTION (EA)
A chance to apply earlier than normal. The benefit is that you hear back from colleges sooner than everyone else. If you're accepted during this time, you aren't forced to attend that university, so EAs are "not binding."

## EARLY DECISION (ED)
A chance to apply early to your #1 college. This route is "binding," meaning that if you're admitted, you have to attend this school if your needs are met with the financial aid package that is offered.

**EFC–Expected Family Contribution**
A number that shows how much money a student and their family is eligible to receive. This number is based on income and assets, and comes either from FAFSA or the student's profile.

**FAFSA—Free Application for Federal Student Aid (pronounced the way it's spelled, not "F-A-F-S-A").**
A no-cost application for students to ask for money from the federal government.

## FINANCIAL AID
Money to help pay for college—sometimes it's free, sometimes you have to pay it back. Financial aid can come from many places: the government (federal and state), the school itself, and private organizations. Search online for financial aid opportunities!

## FINANCIAL AID OFFICE
The place at a school that helps students get money.

## FINANCIAL AID PACKAGE
How much money a student will officially get.

**FSA ID—Federal Student Aid Identification**
This ID is a username and password combination. It identifies a student or parent and lets them see personal information in different U.S. Department of Education systems. This ID can be used as a digital signature for online forms.

## GAP YEAR
A year between high school and college. Students choose to take this time to work, volunteer, travel, and/or learn more about themselves. There are agencies that can help place students in gap year programs.

## GED (GENERAL EDUCATIONAL TEST)
A test students can take instead of getting a high school diploma.

**IB** *aka international baccalaureate*
This high school program is recognized by universities worldwide. It includes advanced courses, tests, and special projects. If this program is completed, a student can begin at many universities at the sophomore level. *IB is not offered at every high school in the U.S.

## LETTER OF INTENT
A letter to a recruited student athlete that explains the value of the athletic scholarship and what a student has to do to keep it.

## MASTER'S DEGREE
Solely focuses on one area of knowledge with supportive course(s) to equip and expand one's expertise.

## MAY 1ST NATIONAL REPLY DATE
On this date, members of the National Association for College Admission Counseling (NACAC) require tuition deposits that will not be refunded. Some universities recommend submitting a refundable housing deposit before that date—doing that will show that you're serious about attending that school.

## MERIT AID
Money given based on student's achievements. Not "need" based.

## NAIA *aka National Association of Intercollegiate Athletics*
This is an association (with ~250 members) for college athletics at smaller universities and colleges in the U.S., and two divisions: Division I (one) and Division II (two). The NAIA's Division I is similar to the NCAA Division II. Athletes can get scholarships through the NAIA.

## NATIONAL PORTFOLIO DAYS
A chance for art schools to see and review student's artwork on display at fairs.

## NCAA *aka National Collegiate Athletic Association*
An organization made up of higher education schools that have athletes ranked in Division I (one), II (two), or III (three). Schools with DI and DII athletes offer athletic scholarships, while DIII teams do not. Recruitment and scholarship offerings are regulated.

## NEED-BASED AID
Money you get (scholarships, grants, loans, and work-study) based on individual financial needs reported in FAFSA.

## NET PRICE CALCULATOR
This helps families see if they can get financial aid. If they can, it gives an idea of how much money they'll get.

## PAYMENT PLAN
A setup to pay tuition over a period of time (<1 year) instead of all at once. Not financial aid.

## PH.D. *aka Doctor of Philosophy*
Doctorate program during which the students posits an academic hypothesis and the dissertation includes academic research leading to new knowledge.

Can get after you finish a bachelor's degree (master's degree not required for this). This degree proves you have done research and written a dissertation (long paper) on a topic that creates new information for experts to use.

## PRIORITY DATE *aka The Due Date*
The time and day when something is due. If this is missed, chances are low of being considered. Ex: for entry into a school, a spot in housing, or as a candidate to get financial aid.

## ROLLING ADMISSION
No due date—you are considered as soon as you turn in your application. You often hear back from schools quickly with this application review system.

## SAR
A report with your expected family contribution (EFC) that you get after submitting FAFSA.

## SAT *aka Scholastic Aptitude Test*
Similar to the ACT, without the science part. It tests math, reading, and writing (the essay is required on this one).

## SAT SUBJECT TESTS
These subject-specific tests take one hour to complete, and are useful to demonstrate your academic strengths (no AP courses required). You can take a subject test for English, science, math, languages, and/or history. Another benefit to taking these optional tests is that at some schools they help with admission decisions. If you do well on a subject test, you may test out of some freshman and general education requirements!

## TOEFL
This standardized test is for English learners to determine their level of English. Many universities (where the majority of courses are taught in English) accept this test.

## TRANSFER STUDENT
A student who goes to a four-year college after finishing their first two years at a different college.

## UNDERGRADUATE
A student who is en route to finish a two-year or four-year degree.

## UNIVERSITY
An institution that consists of "colleges/schools" within that may include graduate degree programs.

## VERBAL COMMITMENT
A promise between a recruited student athlete and a university coach that guarantees a student will attend that school. This usually happens before the student is allowed to sign a letter of intent.

## WAITING LIST
A list of applicants who might get into a college if a spot opens up after everyone who is accepted decides whether or not to attend.

## WEIGHTED GRADE POINT AVERAGE (GPA)
A way to calculate your grade point average that includes how hard the classes were. Ex: an "A" in an advanced placement (AP) class is worth more than in a regular class. Check this out to learn how to convert your GPA to a 4.0 scale.

LIFE

_____

_____

_____

_____

CAREER

_____

_____

_____

_____

## EDUCATION

_____

_____

_____

_____

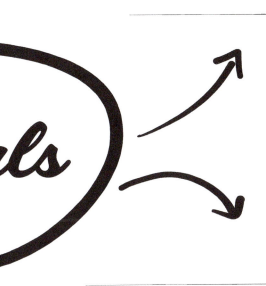

## ACTIVITIES

_____

_____

_____

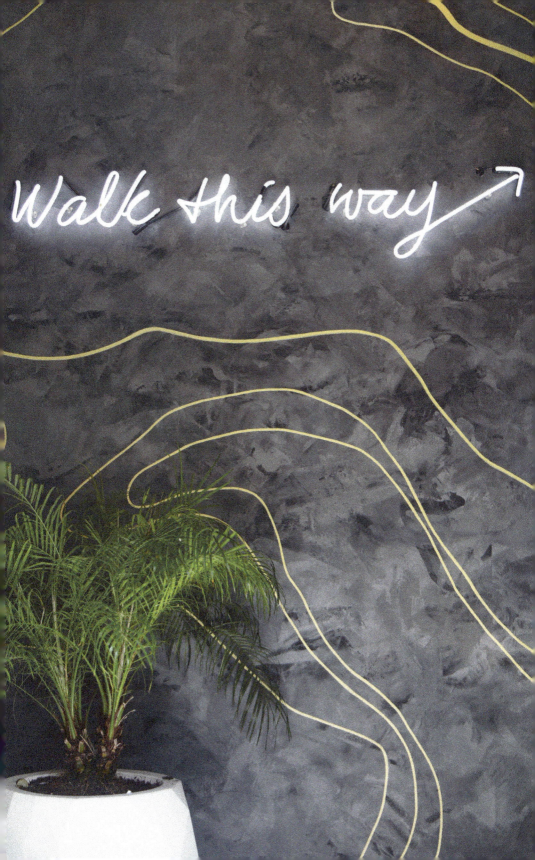

# Your Timeline

## JUNIOR YEAR

| JANUARY - FEBRUARY | MARCH | APRIL |
|---|---|---|

**MARCH**
- [ ] Create college list
- [ ] Begin college visits
- [ ] Apply for academic opportunities

**APRIL**
- [ ] Attend college fairs
- [ ] Register for AP exams
- [ ] Look into summer involvement

**JANUARY - FEBRUARY**
- [ ] Register for the ACT and/or SAT
- [ ] Meet with your counselor for Senior registration and College exploration

| OCTOBER - NOVEMBER | DECEMBER |
|---|---|

**OCTOBER - NOVEMBER**
- [ ] Apply for FAFSA
- [ ] Send in your ACT/SAT scores and high school transcript
- [ ] Complete all of your applications and put the finishing touches on your college essays
- [ ] Seek other scholarships

**DECEMBER**
- [ ] Focus on academics

# SENIOR YEAR

☐ College essay prep

☐ Request letters of recommendation

☐ Visit colleges

☐ Create a master list of 10-12 or your chosen colleges

☐ Create accounts for college applications

☐ Update resume

☐ Narrow and shape college list

☐ Visit colleges

☐ Job or volunteer opportunity

☐ Register for the ACT and/or SAT (2nd time)

☐ Review award letters

☐ Evaluate options and decide

☐ Submit your intent by May 1st

☐ Sign up for orientation

☐ Seek campus housing

☐ Submit final transcripts

☐ Decision notifications

☐ Manage student portals

☐ Follow waitlist instructions

☐ Attend admitted student events

# ADVISOR TO DO LIST

Meeting with an advisor is extremely important. An advisor could be a school counselor, a teacher, an administrator, or a parent (or someone who has been to college). When you meet with your advisor, make a list of things they want you to do. (This way you'll remember what you talked about later on.)

- [ ] _____
- [ ] _____
- [ ] _____
- [ ] _____
- [ ] _____
- [ ] _____
- [ ] _____
- [ ] _____
- [ ] _____
- [ ] _____

# Resources

| RESOURCE NAME | LOCATION |
| --- | --- |
| | |
| | |
| | |
| | |
| | |
| | |
| | |
| | |
| | |
| | |
| | |
| | |
| | |

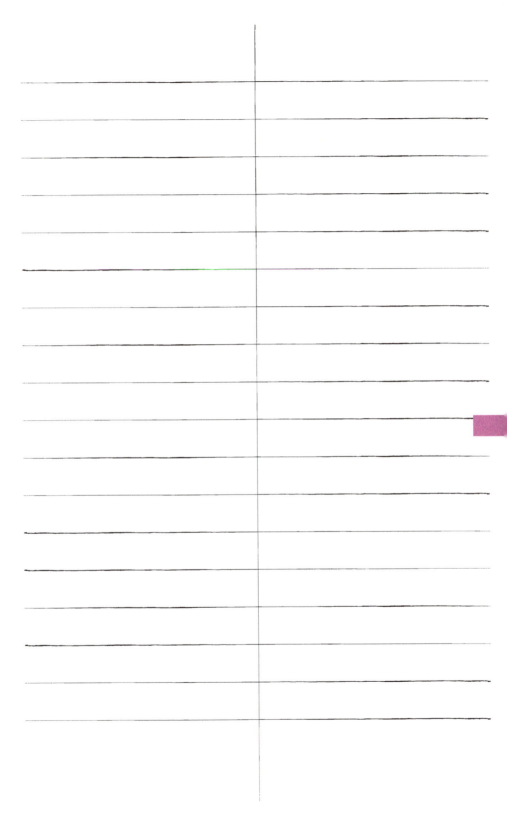

Steal Like An
Artist

BOOKS

I AM
AN ARTIST

THE POWER
OF WHY

HIRE-OUT
CLIMBING

C

RUNNI
AND IDE

COACHING

# College List

As you make/create your college list, you want to find colleges/universities that are a good fit. Consider factors like location, cost, if your desired major is offered, and what the campus culture is like.

_____

_____

_____

_____

_____

_____

_____

_____

_____

_____

_____

_____

_____

_____

_____

_____

# CHOOSE YOUR TOP 12

Another factor to include when making your list is to look at the acceptance rate. A good strategy is to apply to 3 types of schools: **"reach,"** **"possible,"** and **"likely"** schools.

- **Reach** schools are very selective — the acceptance rate is less than 25%
- **Possible** schools are somewhat selective — the acceptance rate is between 25% to 50%
- **Likely** schools are less selective — the acceptance rate is more than 50%

Apply to at least one in every category.

| COLLEGE NAME | APP DUE DATE | R/P/L |
|---|---|---|
|  |  |  |
|  |  |  |
|  |  |  |
|  |  |  |
|  |  |  |
|  |  |  |
|  |  |  |
|  |  |  |
|  |  |  |
|  |  |  |
|  |  |  |
|  |  |  |

# COLLEGE NAME: University xyz

Campus Visit, College Fair, Presentation, Web/Book

## TYPE:
- [X] Public
- [ ] Private
- [ ] Other

4 year

## LOCATION:
- [X] City
- [ ] Suburban
- [ ] Small town

San Jose, Ca

## ENROLLMENT:
Undergraduate

30,609

Graduate

11,615

## ADMISSIONS INFO:

Early Action Date: Nov 1

Early Decision:

Regular Decision: Jan 1

GPA Average: 3.75

Test Average: ACT 30-34

## RETENTION:

Return for sophomore year

97%

Graduating in 6 years percentage

92%

## ACCEPTED APPLICANTS PERCENTAGE: 17%

(25% Very Selective)   26% – 50% Selective   >50% Less Selective

## MAJOR/MINOR INTERESTS:
Social Sciences
Engineering
Business

## CAMPUS INVOLVEMENT:
Organizations, clubs, sports, etc.

RHA

Intramural Sports

Film Society

Student Newspaper

## COST OF ATTENDANCE:
- [X] In-State
- [ ] Out-of-State

Tuition/Fees: $10,805

Housing: $6,500

Meal Plan: $4,500

Books & Supplies: $700

Personal Expenses: $2,910

Transportation Expenses: $1,490

Other: $800

**Total:** 27,705

# COLLEGE NAME: _____

Campus Visit, College Fair, Presentation, Web/Book

**TYPE:**

☐ Public

☐ Private

☐ Other

**LOCATION:**

☐ City

☐ Suburban

☐ Small town

**ENROLLMENT:**

Undergraduate

_____

Graduate

_____

**ADMISSIONS INFO:**

Early Action Date: _____

Early Decision: _____

Regular Decision: _____

GPA Average: _____

Test Average: _____

**RETENTION:**

Return for
sophomore year

Graduating in 6
years percentage

_____     _____

| **ACCEPTED APPLICANTS PERCENTAGE:** | 25%<br>Very Selective | 26% – 50%<br>Selective | >50%<br>Less Selective |
|---|---|---|---|

**MAJOR/MINOR INTERESTS:**

_____

_____

_____

**CAMPUS INVOLVEMENT:**
Organizations, clubs, sports, etc.

_____

_____

_____

**COST OF ATTENDANCE:**

☐ In-State    ☐ Out-of-State

Tuition/Fees:

Housing:

Meal Plan:

Books & Supplies:

Personal Expenses:

Transportation Expenses:

Other:

**Total:** _____

# COLLEGE NAME: _____

Campus Visit, College Fair, Presentation, Web/Book

**TYPE:**
- [ ] Public
- [ ] Private
- [ ] Other

**LOCATION:**
- [ ] City
- [ ] Suburban
- [ ] Small town

**ENROLLMENT:**
Undergraduate
_____

Graduate
_____

**ADMISSIONS INFO:**

Early Action Date: _____

Early Decision: _____

Regular Decision: _____

GPA Average: _____

Test Average: _____

**RETENTION:**

Return for
sophomore year

Graduating in 6
years percentage

_____    _____

**ACCEPTED APPLICANTS PERCENTAGE:**

| 25% | 26% - 50% | >50% |
|---|---|---|
| Very Selective | Selective | Less Selective |

**MAJOR/MINOR INTERESTS:**

_____

_____

_____

**CAMPUS INVOLVEMENT:**
Organizations, clubs, sports, etc.

_____

_____

_____

_____

**COST OF ATTENDANCE:**
- [ ] In-State   [ ] Out-of-State

Tuition/Fees: _____

Housing: _____

Meal Plan: _____

Books & Supplies: _____

Personal Expenses: _____

Transportation Expenses: _____

Other: _____

**Total:** _____

# COLLEGE NAME: _____

Campus Visit, College Fair, Presentation, Web/Book

**TYPE:**
- ☐ Public
- ☐ Private
- ☐ Other

**LOCATION:**
- ☐ City
- ☐ Suburban
- ☐ Small town

**ENROLLMENT:**

Undergraduate

_____

Graduate

**ADMISSIONS INFO:**

Early Action Date: _____

Early Decision: _____

Regular Decision: _____

GPA Average: _____

Test Average: _____

**RETENTION:**

Return for sophomore year

Graduating in 6 years percentage

_____    _____

**ACCEPTED APPLICANTS PERCENTAGE:**

| 25% | 26% - 50% | >50% |
|-----|-----------|------|
| Very Selective | Selective | Less Selective |

**MAJOR/MINOR INTERESTS:**

_____

_____

_____

**CAMPUS INVOLVEMENT:**
Organizations, clubs, sports, etc.

_____

_____

_____

_____

**COST OF ATTENDANCE:**

☐ In-State   ☐ Out-of-State

Tuition/Fees:

Housing:

Meal Plan:

Books & Supplies:

Personal Expenses:

Transportation Expenses:

Other:

**Total:** _____

# COLLEGE NAME: _____

Campus Visit, College Fair, Presentation, Web/Book

**TYPE:**
- ☐ Public
- ☐ Private
- ☐ Other

**LOCATION:**
- ☐ City
- ☐ Suburban
- ☐ Small town

**ENROLLMENT:**
Undergraduate

_____

Graduate

_____

**ADMISSIONS INFO:**

Early Action Date: _____

Early Decision: _____

Regular Decision: _____

GPA Average: _____

Test Average: _____

**RETENTION:**

Return for sophomore year

Graduating in 6 years percentage

_____       _____

**ACCEPTED APPLICANTS PERCENTAGE:**

| 25% | 26% – 50% | >50% |
|-----|-----------|------|
| Very Selective | Selective | Less Selective |

**MAJOR/MINOR INTERESTS:**

_____

_____

_____

**CAMPUS INVOLVEMENT:**
Organizations, clubs, sports, etc.

_____

_____

_____

_____

**COST OF ATTENDANCE:**
☐ In-State   ☐ Out-of-State

Tuition/Fees:

Housing:

Meal Plan:

Books & Supplies:

Personal Expenses:

Transportation Expenses:

Other:

**Total:** _____

# COLLEGE NAME: _____

Campus Visit, College Fair, Presentation, Web/Book

**TYPE:**

☐ Public

☐ Private

☐ Other

**LOCATION:**

☐ City

☐ Suburban

☐ Small town

**ENROLLMENT:**

Undergraduate

_____

Graduate

_____

**ADMISSIONS INFO:**

Early Action Date: _____

Early Decision: _____

Regular Decision: _____

GPA Average: _____

Test Average: _____

**RETENTION:**

Return for sophomore year

_____

Graduating in 6 years percentage

_____

**ACCEPTED APPLICANTS PERCENTAGE:**

| 25% | 26% - 50% | >50% |
|---|---|---|
| Very Selective | Selective | Less Selective |

**MAJOR/MINOR INTERESTS:**

_____

_____

_____

**CAMPUS INVOLVEMENT:**
Organizations, clubs, sports, etc.

_____

_____

_____

_____

**COST OF ATTENDANCE:**

☐ In-State   ☐ Out-of-State

Tuition/Fees:

Housing:

Meal Plan:

Books & Supplies:

Personal Expenses:

Transportation Expenses:

Other:

**Total:** _____

# COLLEGE NAME: _____

Campus Visit, College Fair, Presentation, Web/Book

**TYPE:**
- ☐ Public
- ☐ Private
- ☐ Other

**LOCATION:**
- ☐ City
- ☐ Suburban
- ☐ Small town

**ENROLLMENT:**
Undergraduate

_____

Graduate

**ADMISSIONS INFO:**

Early Action Date: _____

Early Decision: _____

Regular Decision: _____

GPA Average: _____

Test Average: _____

**RETENTION:**

Return for sophomore year

Graduating in 6 years percentage

_____     _____

**ACCEPTED APPLICANTS PERCENTAGE:**

| 25% | 26% – 50% | >50% |
|-----|-----------|------|
| Very Selective | Selective | Less Selective |

**MAJOR/MINOR INTERESTS:**

_____

_____

_____

**CAMPUS INVOLVEMENT:**
Organizations, clubs, sports, etc.

_____

_____

_____

_____

**COST OF ATTENDANCE:**
- ☐ In-State   ☐ Out-of-State

Tuition/Fees:

Housing:

Meal Plan:

Books & Supplies:

Personal Expenses:

Transportation Expenses:

Other:

**Total:** _____

# COLLEGE NAME: _____

Campus Visit, College Fair, Presentation, Web/Book

**TYPE:**
- ☐ Public
- ☐ Private
- ☐ Other

**LOCATION:**
- ☐ City
- ☐ Suburban
- ☐ Small town

**ENROLLMENT:**
Undergraduate

_____

Graduate

**ADMISSIONS INFO:**

Early Action Date: _____

Early Decision: _____

Regular Decision: _____

GPA Average: _____

Test Average: _____

**RETENTION:**

Return for
sophomore year

Graduating in 6
years percentage

_____  _____

**ACCEPTED APPLICANTS
PERCENTAGE:**

| 25% | 26% – 50% | >50% |
|-----|-----------|------|
| Very Selective | Selective | Less Selective |

**MAJOR/MINOR INTERESTS:**

_____

_____

_____

**CAMPUS INVOLVEMENT:**
Organizations, clubs, sports, etc.

_____

_____

_____

_____

**COST OF ATTENDANCE:**

☐ In-State   ☐ Out-of-State

Tuition/Fees:

Housing:

Meal Plan:

Books & Supplies:

Personal Expenses:

Transportation Expenses:

Other:

**Total:** _____

# COLLEGE NAME: _____

Campus Visit, College Fair, Presentation, Web/Book

**TYPE:**
- [ ] Public
- [ ] Private
- [ ] Other

**LOCATION:**
- [ ] City
- [ ] Suburban
- [ ] Small town

**ENROLLMENT:**
Undergraduate

_____

Graduate

_____

**ADMISSIONS INFO:**

Early Action Date: _____

Early Decision: _____

Regular Decision: _____

GPA Average: _____

Test Average: _____

**RETENTION:**

Return for sophomore year

_____

Graduating in 6 years percentage

_____

**ACCEPTED APPLICANTS PERCENTAGE:**

| 25% | 26% - 50% | >50% |
|-----|-----------|------|
| Very Selective | Selective | Less Selective |

**MAJOR/MINOR INTERESTS:**

_____

_____

_____

**CAMPUS INVOLVEMENT:**
Organizations, clubs, sports, etc.

_____

_____

_____

**COST OF ATTENDANCE:**
- [ ] In-State
- [ ] Out-of-State

Tuition/Fees:

Housing:

Meal Plan:

Books & Supplies:

Personal Expenses:

Transportation Expenses:

Other:

**Total:** _____

# COLLEGE NAME: _____

Campus Visit, College Fair, Presentation, Web/Book

**TYPE:**
☐ Public
☐ Private
☐ Other

**LOCATION:**
☐ City
☐ Suburban
☐ Small town

**ENROLLMENT:**
Undergraduate

_____

Graduate

**ADMISSIONS INFO:**

Early Action Date: _____

Early Decision: _____

Regular Decision: _____

GPA Average: _____

Test Average: _____

**RETENTION:**

Return for
sophomore year

_____

Graduating in 6
years percentage

_____

**ACCEPTED APPLICANTS PERCENTAGE:**

| 25% | 26% – 50% | >50% |
|-----|-----------|------|
| Very Selective | Selective | Less Selective |

**MAJOR/MINOR INTERESTS:**

_____

_____

_____

**CAMPUS INVOLVEMENT:**
Organizations, clubs, sports, etc.

_____

_____

_____

**COST OF ATTENDANCE:**
☐ In-State  ☐ Out-of-State

Tuition/Fees:

Housing:

Meal Plan:

Books & Supplies:

Personal Expenses:

Transportation Expenses:

Other:

**Total:** _____

# COLLEGE NAME: _____

Campus Visit, College Fair, Presentation, Web/Book

**TYPE:**
- ☐ Public
- ☐ Private
- ☐ Other

**LOCATION:**
- ☐ City
- ☐ Suburban
- ☐ Small town

**ENROLLMENT:**
Undergraduate

_____

Graduate

**ADMISSIONS INFO:**

Early Action Date: _____

Early Decision: _____

Regular Decision: _____

GPA Average: _____

Test Average: _____

**RETENTION:**

Return for sophomore year

Graduating in 6 years percentage

_____   _____

**ACCEPTED APPLICANTS PERCENTAGE:**

| 25% | 26% – 50% | >50% |
|-----|-----------|------|
| Very Selective | Selective | Less Selective |

**MAJOR/MINOR INTERESTS:**

_____

_____

_____

**CAMPUS INVOLVEMENT:**
Organizations, clubs, sports, etc.

_____

_____

_____

**COST OF ATTENDANCE:**
☐ In-State   ☐ Out-of-State

Tuition/Fees:

Housing:

Meal Plan:

Books & Supplies:

Personal Expenses:

Transportation Expenses:

Other:

**Total:** _____

# COLLEGE NAME: _____

Campus Visit, College Fair, Presentation, Web/Book

**TYPE:**

☐ Public

☐ Private

☐ Other

**LOCATION:**

☐ City

☐ Suburban

☐ Small town

**ENROLLMENT:**

Undergraduate

_____

Graduate

**ADMISSIONS INFO:**

Early Action Date: _____

Early Decision: _____

Regular Decision: _____

GPA Average: _____

Test Average: _____

**RETENTION:**

Return for sophomore year

Graduating in 6 years percentage

_____    _____

| **ACCEPTED APPLICANTS PERCENTAGE:** | **25%** Very Selective | **26% - 50%** Selective | **>50%** Less Selective | |
|---|---|---|---|---|

**MAJOR/MINOR INTERESTS:**

_____

_____

_____

**CAMPUS INVOLVEMENT:**
Organizations, clubs, sports, etc.

_____

_____

_____

**COST OF ATTENDANCE:**

☐ In-State    ☐ Out-of-State

Tuition/Fees:

Housing:

Meal Plan:

Books & Supplies:

Personal Expenses:

Transportation Expenses:

Other:

**Total:** _____

# COLLEGE NAME: _____

Campus Visit, College Fair, Presentation, Web/Book

**TYPE:**
☐ Public
☐ Private
☐ Other

**LOCATION:**
☐ City
☐ Suburban
☐ Small town

**ENROLLMENT:**
Undergraduate
_____

Graduate
_____

**ADMISSIONS INFO:**

Early Action Date: _____

Early Decision: _____

Regular Decision: _____

GPA Average: _____

Test Average: _____

**RETENTION:**

Return for
sophomore year

Graduating in 6
years percentage

_____    _____

**ACCEPTED APPLICANTS
PERCENTAGE:**

| 25% | 26% - 50% | >50% |
| Very Selective | Selective | Less Selective |

**MAJOR/MINOR INTERESTS:**

_____

_____

_____

**CAMPUS INVOLVEMENT:**
Organizations, clubs, sports, etc.

_____

_____

_____

_____

**COST OF ATTENDANCE:**

☐ In-State    ☐ Out-of-State

Tuition/Fees:

Housing:

Meal Plan:

Books & Supplies:

Personal Expenses:

Transportation Expenses:

Other:

**Total:** _____

# COLLEGE NAME: _____

Campus Visit, College Fair, Presentation, Web/Book

**TYPE:**
- ☐ Public
- ☐ Private
- ☐ Other

**LOCATION:**
- ☐ City
- ☐ Suburban
- ☐ Small town

**ENROLLMENT:**
Undergraduate

_____

Graduate

_____

**ADMISSIONS INFO:**

Early Action Date: _____

Early Decision: _____

Regular Decision: _____

GPA Average: _____

Test Average: _____

**RETENTION:**

Return for sophomore year

_____

Graduating in 6 years percentage

_____

**ACCEPTED APPLICANTS PERCENTAGE:**

| 25% | 26% – 50% | >50% |
|-----|-----------|------|
| Very Selective | Selective | Less Selective |

**MAJOR/MINOR INTERESTS:**

_____

_____

_____

**CAMPUS INVOLVEMENT:**
Organizations, clubs, sports, etc.

_____

_____

_____

_____

**COST OF ATTENDANCE:**
- ☐ In-State
- ☐ Out-of-State

Tuition/Fees:

Housing:

Meal Plan:

Books & Supplies:

Personal Expenses:

Transportation Expenses:

Other:

**Total:** _____

# COLLEGE NAME: _____

Campus Visit, College Fair, Presentation, Web/Book

**TYPE:**
- ☐ Public
- ☐ Private
- ☐ Other

**LOCATION:**
- ☐ City
- ☐ Suburban
- ☐ Small town

**ENROLLMENT:**
Undergraduate

_____

Graduate

**ADMISSIONS INFO:**

Early Action Date: _____

Early Decision: _____

Regular Decision: _____

GPA Average: _____

Test Average: _____

**RETENTION:**

Return for
sophomore year

Graduating in 6
years percentage

_____      _____

**ACCEPTED APPLICANTS PERCENTAGE:**

| 25% | 26% – 50% | >50% |
|---|---|---|
| Very Selective | Selective | Less Selective |

**MAJOR/MINOR INTERESTS:**

_____

_____

_____

**CAMPUS INVOLVEMENT:**
Organizations, clubs, sports, etc.

_____

_____

_____

_____

**COST OF ATTENDANCE:**
- ☐ In-State   ☐ Out-of-State

Tuition/Fees:

Housing:

Meal Plan:

Books & Supplies:

Personal Expenses:

Transportation Expenses:

Other:

**Total:** _____

# COLLEGE NAME: _____

Campus Visit, College Fair, Presentation, Web/Book

**TYPE:**

☐ Public

☐ Private

☐ Other

**LOCATION:**

☐ City

☐ Suburban

☐ Small town

**ENROLLMENT:**

Undergraduate

_____

Graduate

_____

**ADMISSIONS INFO:**

Early Action Date: _____

Early Decision: _____

Regular Decision: _____

GPA Average: _____

Test Average: _____

**RETENTION:**

Return for
sophomore year

Graduating in 6
years percentage

_____   _____

**ACCEPTED APPLICANTS PERCENTAGE:**

| 25% | 26% – 50% | >50% |
|---|---|---|
| Very Selective | Selective | Less Selective |

**MAJOR/MINOR INTERESTS:**

_____

_____

_____

**CAMPUS INVOLVEMENT:**

Organizations, clubs, sports, etc.

_____

_____

_____

_____

**COST OF ATTENDANCE:**

☐ In-State   ☐ Out-of-State

Tuition/Fees:

Housing:

Meal Plan:

Books & Supplies:

Personal Expenses:

Transportation Expenses:

Other:

**Total:** _____

DO V
YOU

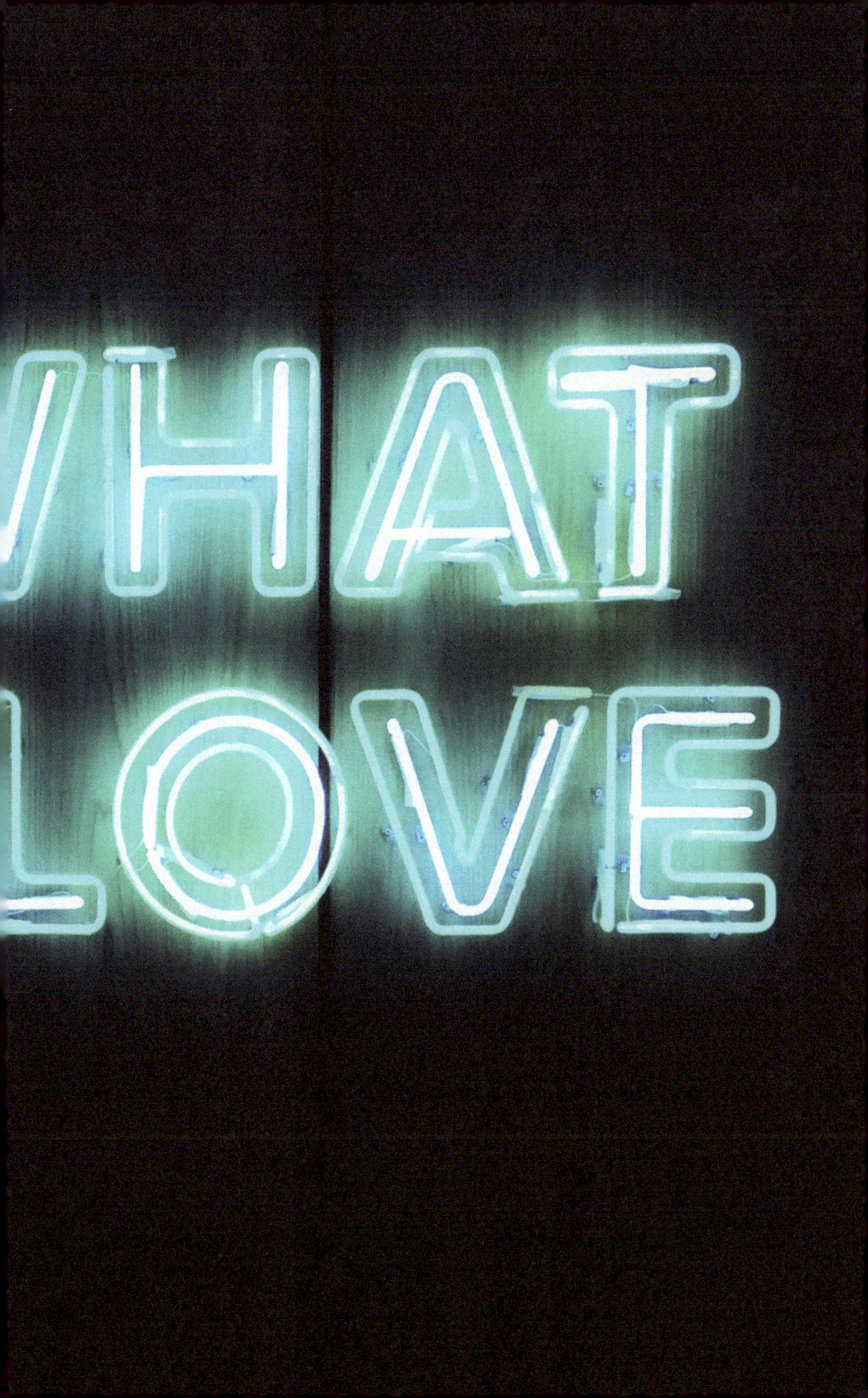
HAT
LOVE

# Highlight Reel

This is your time to think about everything you have been involved in and everything you have accomplished, even if it's not academic. Remember that numbers **stand out**, so use them as much as possible *(ex: "I tutored 3 students 4 hours a week" instead of "I tutored every week")* This is the part where you should brag!

## ACTIVITIES

List school and non-school activities, what role or position you had in the organization, how many hours per week, and (if it applies) years you were involved

_____

_____

_____

_____

_____

## JOBS

List any jobs you had, how long you worked, and how many hours you worked every week on average

_____

_____

_____

_____

## AWARDS

List all of your achievements, from small to big. This can be an award given in class *(ex: "Best Science Project")* or things on a larger, wider-reaching scale *(ex: "placed 4th in the state/regional championship")*.

_____

_____

_____

_____

_____

## VOLUNTEERING

List any volunteering you did, how long you worked, and how many hours you usually worked every week

_____

_____

_____

_____

_____

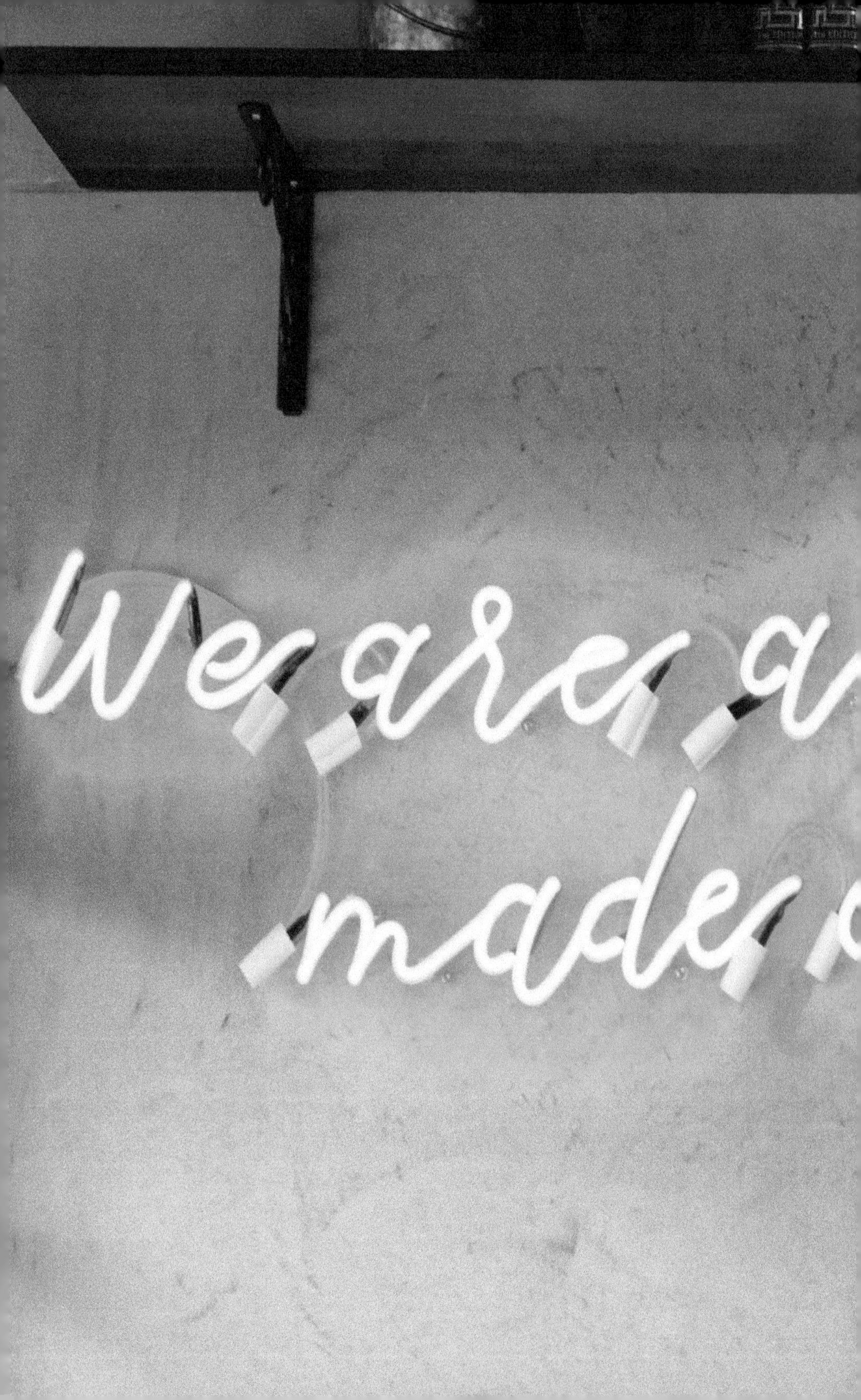
We are
made

# Essay Prep

## ESSAY QUESTION OR TOPIC

COLLEGE:

DUE DATE:

TYPE OF ESSAY:

WORD COUNT:

# Essay Prep

## ESSAY QUESTION OR TOPIC

_____

_____

_____

**COLLEGE:**                          **DUE DATE:**

**TYPE OF ESSAY:**                    **WORD COUNT:**

# Essay Prep

## ESSAY QUESTION OR TOPIC

_____

_____

_____

COLLEGE:                          DUE DATE:

TYPE OF ESSAY:                    WORD COUNT:

# Essay Prep

## ESSAY QUESTION OR TOPIC

_____

_____

_____

**COLLEGE:**                          **DUE DATE:**

**TYPE OF ESSAY:**                    **WORD COUNT:**

# Essay Prep

## ESSAY QUESTION OR TOPIC

_____

_____

_____

COLLEGE:                          DUE DATE:

TYPE OF ESSAY:                    WORD COUNT:

# Essay Prep

## ESSAY QUESTION OR TOPIC

_____

_____

_____

COLLEGE:                              DUE DATE:

TYPE OF ESSAY:                        WORD COUNT:

# Essay Prep

## ESSAY QUESTION OR TOPIC

COLLEGE:

DUE DATE:

TYPE OF ESSAY:

WORD COUNT:

# *Essay Prep*

## ESSAY QUESTION OR TOPIC

_____

_____

_____

**COLLEGE:**                        **DUE DATE:**

**TYPE OF ESSAY:**              **WORD COUNT:**

# Essay Prep

## ESSAY QUESTION OR TOPIC

COLLEGE:                                    DUE DATE:

TYPE OF ESSAY:                              WORD COUNT:

# Essay Prep

## ESSAY QUESTION OR TOPIC

_____

_____

_____

**COLLEGE:**

**DUE DATE:**

**TYPE OF ESSAY:**

**WORD COUNT:**

**MONTH**

**YEAR**

| SUN | MON | TUE | WED | THU | FRI | SAT |
|-----|-----|-----|-----|-----|-----|-----|

**TASKS**

**NOTES**

**MONTH**

**YEAR**

| SUN | MON | TUE | WED | THU | FRI | SAT |
|-----|-----|-----|-----|-----|-----|-----|
|     |     |     |     |     |     |     |

**TASKS**

**NOTES**

**MONTH**

**YEAR**

| SUN | MON | TUE | WED | THU | FRI | SAT |
|-----|-----|-----|-----|-----|-----|-----|
|     |     |     |     |     |     |     |

**TASKS**

**NOTES**

## MONTH

## YEAR

| SUN | MON | TUE | WED | THU | FRI | SAT |
|-----|-----|-----|-----|-----|-----|-----|
|     |     |     |     |     |     |     |

## TASKS

## NOTES

**MONTH**

**YEAR**

| SUN | MON | TUE | WED | THU | FRI | SAT |
|-----|-----|-----|-----|-----|-----|-----|

**TASKS**

**NOTES**

## MONTH

## YEAR

| SUN | MON | TUE | WED | THU | FRI | SAT |
|-----|-----|-----|-----|-----|-----|-----|

NOTES

| | | | MONTH | | | YEAR |
|---|---|---|---|---|---|---|

| SUN | MON | TUE | WED | THU | FRI | SAT |
|-----|-----|-----|-----|-----|-----|-----|
| | | | | | | |

## TASKS

## NOTES

**MONTH** **YEAR**

| SUN | MON | TUE | WED | THU | FRI | SAT |
|-----|-----|-----|-----|-----|-----|-----|

**TASKS**

**NOTES**

| SUN | MON | TUE | WED | THU | FRI | SAT |
|-----|-----|-----|-----|-----|-----|-----|

**TASKS**

**NOTES**

**MONTH**

**YEAR**

| SUN | MON | TUE | WED | THU | FRI | SAT |
|-----|-----|-----|-----|-----|-----|-----|
|     |     |     |     |     |     |     |

**TASKS**

**NOTES**

**MONTH**

**YEAR**

| SUN | MON | TUE | WED | THU | FRI | SAT |
|-----|-----|-----|-----|-----|-----|-----|

**TASKS**

**NOTES**

| SUN | MON | TUE | WED | THU | FRI | SAT |
| --- | --- | --- | --- | --- | --- | --- |
| | | | | | | |

**TASKS**

**NOTES**

**MONTH**

**YEAR**

| SUN | MON | TUE | WED | THU | FRI | SAT |
|-----|-----|-----|-----|-----|-----|-----|

**TASKS**

**NOTES**

| SUN | MON | TUE | WED | THU | FRI | SAT |
|-----|-----|-----|-----|-----|-----|-----|
|     |     |     |     |     |     |     |

**TASKS**

**NOTES**

# MONTH

# YEAR

| SUN | MON | TUE | WED | THU | FRI | SAT |
|-----|-----|-----|-----|-----|-----|-----|

## TASKS

## NOTES

**MONTH**

**YEAR**

| SUN | MON | TUE | WED | THU | FRI | SAT |
|-----|-----|-----|-----|-----|-----|-----|
|     |     |     |     |     |     |     |

**TASKS**

**NOTES**

**MONTH**

**YEAR**

| SUN | MON | TUE | WED | THU | FRI | SAT |
|-----|-----|-----|-----|-----|-----|-----|

**TASKS**

**NOTES**

MONTH

YEAR

| SUN | MON | TUE | WED | THU | FRI | SAT |
|-----|-----|-----|-----|-----|-----|-----|

**TASKS**

**NOTES**

| SUN | MON | TUE | WED | THU | FRI | SAT |
|-----|-----|-----|-----|-----|-----|-----|

**TASKS**

**NOTES**

| SUN | MON | TUE | WED | THU | FRI | SAT |
|-----|-----|-----|-----|-----|-----|-----|
|     |     |     |     |     |     |     |

**TASKS**

**NOTES**

| SUN | MON | TUE | WED | THU | FRI | SAT |
|-----|-----|-----|-----|-----|-----|-----|
|     |     |     |     |     |     |     |

**TASKS**

**NOTES**

| SUN | MON | TUE | WED | THU | FRI | SAT |
|---|---|---|---|---|---|---|
| | | | | | | |

**TASKS**

**NOTES**

| SUN | MON | TUE | WED | THU | FRI | SAT |
|-----|-----|-----|-----|-----|-----|-----|

**TASKS**

**NOTES**

**MONTH**

**YEAR**

| SUN | MON | TUE | WED | THU | FRI | SAT |
|-----|-----|-----|-----|-----|-----|-----|
|     |     |     |     |     |     |     |

**TASKS**

**NOTES**

# COURSES

PROFESSOR / INSTRUCTOR:
TEACHING ASSISTANT:
FRIENDS:
STUDY GROUP:

**EFFORT RATING =**   CHALLENG
HOW HARD WILL I NEED TO            ───────
WORK FOR THE RESULT I WANT?    TALENT

**FINANCIAL**
**ACCOUNTING**   $\boxed{\$ \$}$ $= \dfrac{8}{4} =$

BUT AT
WHAT COST?                $\dfrac{8}{6} = 1.$

TAKES AWAY
FROM SOMETHING
ELSE (STUDY, SOCIAL, WORK)

# DRIVE → HOW AWESOME
DO YOU WANT
TO BE?

# TIME
# TRACKING

HOW MUCH TIME
DO I HAVE? HOW
MUCH DO I NEED?

COURSE A
COURSE B
COURSE C
COURSE D
SOCIAL
WORK
SLEEP/HEALTH

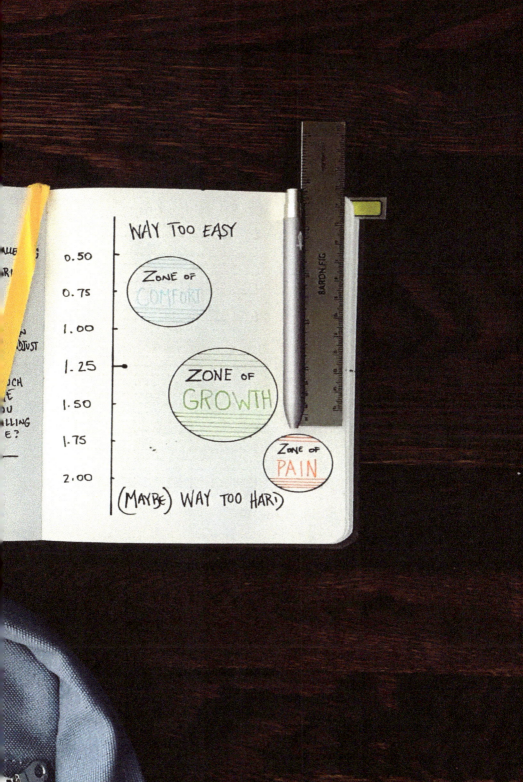